Talk Your Way To The Top

How Professional Service Providers Can Substantially Increase Their Income by Marketing Their Firms Through Seminars.

By

Steve McIntyre-Smith

www.stevemcintyresmith.com

Copyright © 2015 Steve McIntyre-Smith.

All rights reserved, including the right to reproduce this book or portions thereof, in any form.

No part of this text may be reproduced in any form without the express written permission of the author.

Version 2014.12.29

For Salima.

Quotes from delegates who have attended some of Steve's recent seminars.

"I attended the 2013 **'Discover the Gold'** Sessions in Markham and within two weeks had **generated $20,000 in business advisory fees**. Without the course I would not have been able to do this.'

'Fantastic presentation and real life examples'

'One of the best courses I've attended!

Whatever you're paying this guy... triple it!'

'Great passion and enthusiasm. A treat!'

*'**Steve's** Partner Bootcamp was among the best practice management courses I have attended. I appreciated Steve's presentation style; many accounting-related courses can be difficult to stay awake through, but this was not one of them.'*

'Steve kept it interesting and talked about relevant issues for keeping your practice efficient.'

'Thank you for the PD course that you instructed in Vancouver Friday and Saturday. **It was extremely insightful and it truly recharged my entrepreneurial spirit at the firm**, and we will implementing the no Time Sheets policy among many other items.'

'Steve is an extremely knowledgeable expert in the public accounting marketing field, and a very enjoyable presenter.'

'Steve is a fantastic presenter, puts the info across very well & in an entertaining style.'

'Steve was a great presenter and kept it fun. Good practical real world knowledge that can be used immediately.'

'The speaker is awesome. He gives lots of good examples.'

'Instructor very knowledgeable & delivers great stories.

'Great course! Great job keeping us engaged and awake!'

"Best seminar thus far with ICABC'

"Steve is amazing. He should do more PD courses."

"Excellent! I would highly recommend it to individuals contemplating the Partnership role."

"Fantastic presenter, I would gladly attend another of Steve's seminars."

"One of the best ICAA speakers I have ever had"

"Steve is an excellent presenter"

"Enthusiastic, willing to stray off presentation materials to discuss topics of interest.

Index

Introduction	8
Chapter One – Why Seminars?	11
Chapter Two – Ideas for Topics	18
Chapter Three – Where?	24
Chapter Four – When?	28
Chapter Five – Who do you invite?	32
Chapter Six – To Charge or Not?	36
Chapter Seven – Finding Some Suitable Co-Hosts	44
Chapter Eight – Some Tips for Speaking in Public.	50
Chapter Nine – Leveraging Your Talk.	57
About the Author	64
Useful Resources	67

Introduction

I had a lucky break in my career in public accounting.

I worked at several firms who put me through some pretty awesome training on public speaking.

Back in the late 1980's and early 1990's I was fortunate enough to go on courses by Dale Carnegie, Zig Ziglar, Tony Robbins and Brian Tracy and I learned a lot.

Since then I have given hundreds of seminars and spoken to thousands of Accountants around the world.

I have spoken from coast to coast in Canada, and in many other places such as The UK, The USA, Bangladesh, Nassau, Barbados, Australia and Latvia to name a few of the venues where I have stepped up to the podium.

I have been a guest speaker at events hosted by others, as a partner retreat leader for example, I have facilitated professional development courses for the Institute of

Chartered Accountants from coast to coast across Canada, and spoken at national conferences at the Bellagio Hotel in Las Vegas, for example.

These days I also host and stage my own seminars, specifically 'Partner Bootcamp' and 'Discover The Gold Hidden In Your Practice'.

For several years I was 'on tour' with CCH (or Wolters Kluwer as they now prefer to be known by) traveling across the nation talking about how professionals can operate more profitable businesses by leveraging technology.

Each time I have stood up to speak I have never encountered any nerves. There are several reasons why, and I will cover them in this book, and much more.

Don't get me wrong. I'm not perfect. I have made more than my fair share of mistakes when it comes to arranging, hosting and speaking at events.

However, one thing I was always good at was analyzing what went wrong or what could have been done better and learning from those occurrences.

Please do not try to sell from the podium – if you want to be successful at this (there are exceptions, of course). I prefer education without obligation as a more subtle method of generating revenue from speaking, but we'll get into that as you continue reading.

Suffice to say that the skill to do comes from doing, and I therefore encourage you to seek out as many speaking opportunities as possible.

The more experience you gain, the better you will become at speaking in public until you too can Talk Your Way to the Top!

Sincerely

Steve McIntyre-Smith

Steve McIntyre-Smith
Toronto, Ontario, Canada. January 2015.

Chapter One – Why Seminars?

'Sell me this pen!'

If you are a pen manufacturer or wholesaler, you can send a sales representative out into the big bad world with some samples and see if they can sell any.

As a part of the cost of doing business you will probably give away a number of free samples to allow buyers to try your product out before deciding if (and how many) they want to buy.

They can take your pen in their hand, write cheques, sign documents and wander around the office with it neatly tucked into their breast pocket. If it doesn't give them blisters, if the cap seals tightly and keeps the nib airtight, and if it doesn't leak in their pocket, then you may well be able to sell them some if the price is right.

Selling pens is easy – you can leave a free sample and come back the next week to take an order.

With professional services, we have no way

of doing that.

We cannot leave a sample of an intangible service, especially one that is consumed at the point of delivery such as accounting, tax, legal, design and consulting services.

But by holding a seminar we can do the next best thing.

Your audience will be looking at you as you deliver your presentation and they'll be thinking:

- Do I like this person? (You)

- Do they know their stuff?

- How well do they handle questions?

- Does his or her firm offer a better alternative than my existing advisors?

- Can I see myself working with this person?

So your job is to quickly earn your audience's trust, get them to like you and want to know more.

Your role is to be a great ambassador for your firm.

Remember, virtually all professional services are about relationships.

It's not about the Law, or the Taxes Act it's not about the designs you deliver or the actual service you provide as a professional.

Technical knowledge is your ticket to get into the game in the first place.

Most (if not all) professional services are about building trust with your client.

We have the – Know me, Like me, Trust me – cycle to navigate before any prospect will decide to buy and become a client.

Seminars are a great way of getting your prospects to warm to you and want to buy from you. They're the closest thing we have to a free sample.

'Microwave Marketing'

The next reason why you really must do some public speaking in order to grow your practice is that we can benefit from the leverage that a seminar affords us.

If you had forty people at your seminar, and your event lasted for two hours, you have marketed your firm to 40 people in two hours

Agreed? Good.

Now, imagine that you had the same 40 people approach you to come out and visit them to discuss an issue and maybe they'll become a client.

If each one took 30 minutes to drive to (and of course, 30 minutes back – we'll ignore geotagging for this example) and your initial meeting was restricted to an hour per, then to see 40 prospects individually would require 80 hours to do so. That's two weeks solid work!

By holding (or appearing as a guest at) a seminar, you can microwave those 80 hours into just two hours – ignoring the preparation time.

That is the second reason why seminars are a great marketing tool.

'Perceived Endorsement'

The third reason why speaking at a seminar is a great marketing tool, and here I am thinking of instances where you might speak at someone else's event, is that you can benefit from the perceived endorsement of the other party whose event you are speaking at.

If a major bank or investment firm or the Board of Trade invite you to speak at one of their events, then those attending will make the connection that the host believes that you and/or your firm are one of the top providers in your marketplace of whatever professional services you provide, as they surely wouldn't invite you into their event if you weren't.

Right?

That's the power of the perceived endorsement. I call it 'Judgment by Association'.

Seminars allow you to piggy-back off the reputation of another organization. But it gets better, much better, as we shall discover later.

'The video connection'

Another reason why you should consider speaking events as a great marketing tool, is that they can be recorded on video.

Once you have your talk on video you can post clips on 'Youtube' and then embed them in your website.

This allows those who could not attend the event to see you in action, and if you do what I do, you could turn them into DVDs and sell them as an additional revenue source.

We will cover this idea in more detail later, but even if you don't go this far, having some clips on 'YouTube' is a really good marketing idea.

'Qualified Leads'

Finally, if you are speaking at a seminar about 'succession planning for family businesses' you already know that those attending are interested in that specific topic.

They may be running a successful family business where the founders are marching towards retirement and they may not be sure what to do for the best.

If the audience is mostly comprised of non clients, then you have a room full of qualified leads to talk to.

Your audience is basically wandering into the venue saying *'I have a succession planning issue and I'm not sure that my present advisors are up to the job'*.

If it is mostly existing clients that are in the audience, then they are already pre-disposed to using you, now this is your opportunity to sell them some additional services.

If you market the event the right way, then you should have an audience of not just qualified leads to speak to, but they may likely be 'hot' leads to sell to.

Now, who wouldn't want that?

Chapter Two – Ideas for Topics

'What if they threw a war and nobody showed up?'

One of the biggest mistakes Lawyers, Banks, Accountants, Investment Advisors and many other professionals make is that they pick a topic that is of great interest to them, but not to their clients or prospects.

In some cases the topic could be of tremendous interest to potential clients, but the firm delivering the seminar has no idea how to properly promote it.

Let's look at a few examples of seminar titles;

- Tax Planning Opportunities For The Family Business

- This Year's Budget & What It Means To You

- Planning Your Retirement

- Profit Improvement Opportunities For Owner-Operators

I think you'll agree that the aforementioned seminar titles are not very exciting, are they?

So let's stage the exact same four seminars and give them a different title.

- **Honey I Shrank The Tax Bill.** *(Some perfectly legal tax strategies the tax man doesn't want you to know)*

- **New Tax Loopholes to Exploit Before The Tax Man Catches On.** *(As created by the latest budget)*

- **How To Laugh All The Way To The Bank In Your Twilight Years.** *(And live the retirement lifestyle you've always dreamed of)*

- **Discover The Gold Hidden In Your Family Business.** *(Make more money next year with little effort)*

Now, be honest, which set of four titles would you be more interested in attending?

Remember, they are exactly the same presentations, the same speakers, the same slides; it's just the title of the seminar that has changed, nothing else.

There will be times, of course, when we have to 'tone it down a little' for some reason or another.

Maybe you are a guest speaker at an organization who would not appreciate you talking about firing 'Pain In The Ass Clients'.

Don't laugh - it's a real example from my own work. I couldn't get the CPAs' professional body interested in a course with that title. No surprises there I guess.

However, I still did the seminar (For a Bank, to their Accountant contacts) and I now (of course) have the DVD of that presentation in my library of DVDs for sale.

So how do you go about picking a title for a presentation you want to stage?

Well for me personally, I work in one of two ways.

1. I will write the presentation with a 'working' (read boring) title and then, when the slides are finished and I have a better feeling for the content, the title often writes itself.

2. Other times I will come up with what I think is a great title, and then write the seminar content based on only that.

It's a personal choice and neither is wrong or right, it's what works best for you that is important.

There are some popular methods to use to create a title, and I'll share them with you here.

'Six Appeal'

1. **Use the "how to" model and offer a Benefit statement:**

    For example, *"How to make more money and pay less tax next year."*

2. **Ask an open-ended question the audience cannot answer:**

    For example, *"What are the three things all successful businesses have in common?"*

3. **Use curiosity:**

    For example, *"Learn the three secrets to a great business plan and have your bank offering to lend you more money to grow"*

4. **Use a vivid statistic:**

    "55% of new businesses fail in their first three years – find out how to avoid their mistakes."

5. **Make an outrageous - but supportable - claim:**

    Such as *"Find an extra $100,000 profits presently hidden in your manufacturing business."*

6. **The Field Test:**

    Write one seminar title per index card. Show them to a friend. Do not ask which one is best. Instead ask, **"Which seminar would you want to hear more about?"** The seminar title they want to hear more about, is the title you need to use.

There is no shortage of ideas for topics for seminars.

Not all of them are good, of course, but now I hope that you will be able to use your creativity and imagination a little more when thinking of titles or subtitles for future events that you will be holding.

Chapter Three – Where?

'Location, location, location.'

Where should you speak?

- Rotary & Similar Organizations
- Board of Trade
- Chamber of Commerce
- Hold Your Own Seminars
- Trade Associations and Professional Bodies
- Online - Webinars

There are many choices of venue, some good and some, well, let's just call them not so good.

If you mare speaking at someone else's event, the venue is set for you, and there is not much you can do about it. But if you are going to venture out and host some of your own events you have a lot of work to do to get the right venue.

ALWAYS check out the venue yourself. Yep, that means getting off your backside and driving to the venues being considered for your event. Sorry, but there's no other way of putting it.

Sure, you could send someone from your office to do it, but I don't recommend it.

There's nothing so reassuring on the day than being totally comfortable in the environment you've chosen to speak at, and you can only do that by having been there before and seen the venue for yourself.

Most hotels have a team dedicated to running events, so they are the people you will want to work closely with to make sure your seminar is a roaring success.

They will usually have a selction of menus to choose from with wide and varied budgets.

Some will charge for the room hire, others will not provided you ensure a minimum number for food and beverages.

Some will have their own Audio/Video technicians, but I find these days that most hotels subcontract that out to a local A/V specialist company, and that usually works well.

Here are some items to consider that could help you make a decision if one venue or another might be better for your event:

- Check for ease of access from major highways

- Check for any known or planned construction on the roads and at the venue during your event

- Parking – how many spots do they have? Is there a charge to delegates for parking and if so, how much?

- Tea/Coffee facilities and catering options

- Check room size, acoustics, seating

- A/V facilities/Projector/Screen

- Washrooms – location relative to the room your event will be in.

- Seating comfort in the room itself –

some hotels have seating that is very uncomfortable to sit in for more than half an hour, while others have very comfy seats. Sit in one of these chairs yourself and make a judgment call.

- Bates' Motel may look like an ideal venue on the web! Always check out the venue yourself.

Chapter Four – When?

'Timing is everything.'

When should you hold your seminar?

Avoid Mondays and Fridays wherever possible – there is a notable decline in attendances on these days due to people taking long weekends and being at the start or end of the week.

Stick to Tuesday, Wednesday or Thursday for best results.

> Generally, the best time of day to hold a seminar is at 6:00 pm. This gives sufficient time for your attendees to leave work, pick up guests and safely drive to the seminar location.
>
> **NOTE:** Retirees over 65 may have a fear of driving at night and don't usually have conflicts with work. If you're holding a seminar aimed at Seniors (such as a succession planning seminar) try a 4:00 pm seminar time (in the summer) or earlier in the Winter and watch your response rates soar!

There are many options to consider, but here are the ones that work best for me:

- Early – 8am & include breakfast
- Daytime – 10am – finish at Noon
- Afternoon – 4pm, skip work early and join us
- Evening – 6pm or later

Each option has its pro's and con's. It depends on your budget and what you want to achieve.

If you have a modest budget - my recomendation for beginners - I'd suggest a 10am start. That way it's too late for breakfast and if you plan your seminar to be between an hour and ninety minutes then there is no need to provide lunch.

However, if you want to impress people, then I would suggest an 8am start with a good breakfast.

Another benefit of an early start is that your no shows will be lower in number as none will have gone into their office first and got distracted and decided not to attend.

No shows are a part of life on the speaking circuit and anything you can do to reduce this helps. If you are charging people to attend you may well find that your numbers are lower, but the quality of those attending is higher.

If you are charging a fee, then your content had better be worth the investment. On the other side of that same coin, charging a fee may mean that you can market via seminars and make a profit at it, instead of it being a cost. More on this later.

You will know your intended delegate profile much better and I, so use your best judgment as to what time of day would work best.

For my typical 2 hour seminar I find 6pm works best. Most people will have had dinner before coming out, and you can get away with just tea or coffee or soft drinks for refreshments, keeping the budget low.

I have also had terrific success with 6pm sessions with Dinner included for high-end clients and prospects who are used to being very well looked after at such events. However, usually in such circumstances I am charging $140 to $200 per hed to attend with their meal included (typically around $60 cost) with a cash bar for alcohol.

Balance that with your budget for food and beverages and your preferred time will often select itself.

Chapter Five – Who do you invite?

'I should never wish to join a club that would have me as a member'

There is no point in having a room full of people who could NEVER buy your services.

We want **PROSPECTS'** bums on seats, right?

Invite clients who could benefit from your additional services but haven't bought yet and get them to bring along a buddy (another potential client).

Don't overlook referral sources – they are a good potential source of clients and this is a good way to keep in touch with them & show-off your expertise.

Back in my day, I would have to buy a list of suitable prospects from a list broker, write an actual letter and write/design an invite that would more often that not be physically printed.

When all the direct mail pieces were printed, it would be a heck of a job to stuff envelopes and co-ordinate everything to get the invites out in the post.

How primitive it all seems today.

When I host my own seminars I don't have to do any of that, thank goodness.

My weapon of choice is a service called Constant Contact and they host my database on the cloud. I use their software to design my own invite on the cloud and they then send out the invites for me by email.

This is a fantastic service that allows me to send out superbly professional invites to around ten thousand people in my newsletter database at no cost to me (other than my Constant Contact Monthly subscription fee of $105 (US) per month).

I set up a payment page for my event within Constant Contact and link it to my credit card processor (PayPal) and I'm all done!

I host events where I charge anything from $89 per person to $1,495 per person, and it works like a dream.

Now, I get nothing for mentioning Constant

Contact within these pages, I just like to point my readers in the right direction and get them enjoying some success as soon as possible.

Try it out – they offer a free trial.

So, back to the point of this chapter, who to invite to your seminar.

The Importance of a good list. This is one of the make or break issues. You have to invite the right people. A list of 100,000 business people in your area may sound interesting, but how recent is the list? Does it have email addresses? How up to date are they?

What businesses are they in? There's no point in inviting people to your seminar who are in industries that you have absolutely no interest in working with.

Use a quality list broker if you have to buy a list and ask them as many questions as you can think of.

At the end of the day there is no list like your own.

Your own Clients, contacts and newsletter subscribers will be the best quality, most up to date and most relevant people to connect with first of all.

Don't forget your network of Bankers, Commercial Real Estate Agents & Lawyers and those who you have met at Board of Trade/Chamber of Commerce meetings in the past.

But your best list is your list of existing clients, especially if you encourage them to bring a friend along.

Chapter Six – To Charge or Not?

'Show me the money!'

There are four main reasons to consider charging a registration fee for your event:

a) Paid events will often generate more actual attendance than free events.

b) Paid events tend to have significantly fewer no-shows than free events.

c) The quality of attendees tends to be higher at paid events

d) You could cover your costs or even make a profit from these events.

There are certain times when you absolutely should not charge a fee. These are mostly when the event is somewhat self-promotional and is looking to educate delegates about your services.

However, there are other times when a registration fee could easily be justified, and we'll get to that shortly, but before we do, let's look at a more typical situation first.

If you want to promote a service, let's say that you're a Lawyer and you want to sell more will writing services.

You might come up with an interesting title such as 'Sixteen Tips to Cut the Government out of your Will and Pass the maximum amount onto your family'.

You get a list of 5,000 or so Seniors in your area and invite them along to your seminar with a free will clinic to be held after.

Anyone who attends your free seminar will get a free consultation (an in-take meeting for their will) over the next few days and you and an assistant will stay behind to get the details of those who want to sign up to get their will written. You might even offer a special Senior's rate for those who attend.

You might even hold the event at the local Seniors' Centre.

Let's say 60 sign up for the seminar, and 50 of them show up on the day.

If your content is good, you may well have 20 new clients waiting for you after the seminar has finished to book their initial meeting with you.

Now you have 20 new cases to process for a will at a discounted rate of say $250 as a flat fee.

20 times $250 is, of course, $5,000 in fees you've now generated from this one event, but wait.

Most of these seniors have homes and some of them may well be sold in the coming years. Who do you think they are going to call when they come to sell their homes? (I'll give you a clue, it's not Ghostbusters!)

If 10 of them come to sell their houses, and if you charge, say $850 per client for that type of transaction, now you have generated an additional $8,500 in fees, bringing the revenue directly attributable to the seminar up to $13,500

If the venue charged you $500 to rent their facility and you spent $10 per head on refreshments, and $1,500 on your list, then you've made $11,500 net from your 2 hour presentation.

Do that six times a year, and now you're looking at netting $69,000 annually from seminar activities. Not too shabby.

What if you charged $25 per person to attend, with the ticket cost deducted from your fee for doing the will? Here's what the numbers would look like:

60 who booked x $25 = $1,500

50 catered for x $10 = $500

Venue rental = $500

Profit from Seminar = $500

Will Writing Revenues generated = $5,000

Total Revenues generated = $5,500

Less Redeemed vouchers (20 x $25) = $500

Net Profit from event = $5,000

PLUS additional conveyance fees = $8,500

$13,500

If you did this six times annually, you would have $81,000 net income generated from your seminars, all things being equal. I have seen, first hand, how this works in practice with a Lawyer I know well.

So now you can see the benefits of even very small seminars generating interesting numbers for you.

But it gets better.

Let's say you're an Accountant who does Forensic accounting and loss of earnings claims.

Lawyers can be a very good source of business for you in cases where they need to bring in an Accountant as an expert witness to quantify their clients' losses or damages.

You might like to develop a national (or regional) network of friendly Lawyers who could pass you litigation support files.

How might you do that?

Why not put on a seminar just for litigation Lawyers?

Maybe the seminar explains a number of key issues to be considered when quantifying damages, and give them an insight into how such calculations are made. (They'll never try to do this themselves!)

Like Accountants, Lawyers have to acquire a certain minimum number of 'Professional Development' hours each year to demonstrate to their own professional body that they are keeping up to date.

Most courses offering 'PD' points are expensive – for the sake of this illustration, let's say $600 per day.

Why not develop a seminar entitled 'Quantifying Damages – A Forensic Accountant's Exposé of the Process for Lawyers'?

The next step would be to get the Law Society to review the content of the presentation for the purpose of getting approval for the award of PD points to any Lawyer who takes the course.

If successful, you, as the Accountant in question, could be sitting on a gold mine. How do I know this? Because I have done it myself. Not when I was in public accounting, but after I had sold my own firm, with one of the first firms I worked with in a marketing role in the UK.

I have just described precisely what they did.

They staged a series of Seminars across the UK, including two back-to-back sold-out sessions at the Law Society in Chancery Lane, London, where they spoke to 400 Lawyers in one day. Talk about leverage!

Funnily enough, the tour cost them nothing to do, as they charged £99 per person and around three or four months after visiting any given City, they would start to see litigation support files come in from lawyers who attended the seminar in that City.

Wonderful stuff.

To summarize, I would say start small, build some confidence in doing this, and don't charge for attending these events just yet. Then, pick a market that has the need for PD points, develop an educational seminar and get the professional body's approval for PD points, then start charging and you'll turn a marketing cost into a revenue stream, and you'll also probably start generating more work in that field if things go well and your seminar has valuable content.

Chapter Seven – Finding Some Suitable Co-Hosts

'Hell, there are no rules here - we're trying to accomplish something.'

If you are not charging for attending your seminar, a neat way to host a seminar for half price, is to find another professional firm to partner with and split the costs.

It also doubles the exposure you get, as the other party might also bring along their own clients, contacts, friends and associates too, and promote the event to their own lists, so it's a win-win situation.

Good professional services partners:

- Accountants
- Bankers
- Lawyers
- Investment Advisors
- Insurance Brokers

It's not a comprehensive list at all, but one

that I have used with much success when I was in Public Accounting.

Once I had found an independent financial advisor whose work and advice I trusted (I even took his advice myself) I was happy to hold a seminar with him and his team. Indeed, this was back in the late 1980's and as far as I can recall, was the very first seminar I spoke at.

God I was awful!

But the content was good and people forgave me my 'ums and ahs' and pregnant pauses while my brain caught up with my mouth during my presentation.

I forget the name of the seminar now, or the topic I spoke about, but I do recall generating over £10,000 in new business from that one evening. That was a decent amount of money back then.

That was what got me started down this public speaking path, and I've never looked back.

I had split the costs of the event with the

investment brokerage, so the event cost me less than £500. I generated a return on investment of 20 to 1. Not bad for a rookie, eh?

If you look at the lifetime value of a client, then the return is significantly higher.

I have a client in Calgary who is a sole practitioner, with no employees, who uses seminars to promote his firm. So, if you are a solo practitioner, don't tell me 'I'm too small to market by seminars'. I don't buy it. Let me tell you how he does it.

He is sole practitioner who went one stage further, and now he simply shows up at a Bank's seminar five or six times a year as a guest speaker and he generates more work for his consulting business than he knows what to do with.

Here's how it happened.

He had a lucky break for this to happen, but we all need a little luck along the journey. I actually believe that we make our own luck.

I am not sure who this quote is really

attributable to: *"The harder I work, the luckier I get."* Some say Gary Player, others say Vince Lombardi and some advocate that Vidaal Sasoon was first to say it. Who cares?

It's a great quote and one that I often use in my own seminars. My point is that luck plays a part in our own careers.

So here's how my client got a lucky break.

He was asked to speak at a Rotary meeting at the last minute, as the scheduled speaker was taken ill on the morning of the day they were due to speak.

The previous speaker that night was dreadfully boring, speaking in a monotone voice, almost sending the crowd to sleep, and then, on comes my client, energetic and fun, vibrant and enthusiastic, he knocks the ball out of the park.

Here's his lucky break.

In the audience was a Banker who did a lot of seminars to promote her Bank. She loved what she saw that night and approached my client with a proposition.

"We do about nine or ten seminars every year around the city. Would you be interested in turning up with your thumb drive and doing what you just did at our seminars?"

Well, what would you do in those circumstances?

Of course, he has been doing this for a few years now, and doesn't really do much marketing at all, as he doesn't need to any more, thanks to these seminars.

This is the equivalent of that Bank say to you (if you were my client in this scenario):

- Don't bother spending the time to find a good venue – we've done that for you.

- Don't go to the expense of buying a list of potential invitees, we have our own that we'll expose your firm to.

- Oh, and don't worry about managing registrations, our people do that.

- Of course, we feed and water the delegates. You don't have to spend a dime on that either.

- Yes, you will also benefit from the perceived endorsement of a Tier One Bank by speaking at our events.
- Yes, we will introduce you to our clients/customers/prospects and we will introduce you to our better clients.

All he has to do now is keep nine days or so free every year and show up with his thumb drive and speak for an hour.

Awesome.

If you can find a good high profile outfit to partner with great things can happen to your practice too.

Chapter Eight – Some Tips for Speaking in Public.

'The human mind is a curious thing – it starts working the moment we are born, but ceases the moment we stand up to speak in public'

If you are starting to speak in public for the first time, I thought I should include a chapter on speaking skills, rather than just throw you into the deep end.

I strongly recommend that you get some professional help as this should not be the only source of advice, but this will set you down the right path.

Twelve tips for speaking in public:

1. **Keep it Professional:** How should you behave and what personality should you assume on stage?

    With a professional and sincere presence, you can establish an immediate trust and respect between you and your audience.

    Over-dress rather than under-dress. A

suit and tie in a business casual event. Business casual in a Jeans & T-Shirt event.

Being just one notch higher than the audience will often set you up as a professional.

2. **Watch your Stance and Posture:** Your stance, the position and bearing of the body while standing, will send a strong message about your self-confidence and credibility as a speaker.

Have a confident stance with legs slightly apart and hands by your sides unless gesturing.

3. **Make Solid Eye Contact:** This one is a difficult one and comes with practice but you should develop a solid eye contact as a good speaker.

Eye contact means that you are talking and connecting with the audience on an individual level.

I call it eye clasp. It's a virtual

handshake – 5 seconds max per person.

4. **Leave your Hands at your Side:** The hardest lesson which seems the most awkward is to have your hands at your sides when you are not gesturing. But that is where they belong.

Never fidget with your hands, making spider hands or Velcro hands or putting them in your pocket, jingling loose change.

Relax. Let them hang by your side unless you are gesturing to make a point.

5. **Use the Right words and No More:** Thomas Jefferson once said:

"The most valuable of all talents is that of never using two words when one will do."

Avoid jargon and filler words such as "ah", "um", "like", "so", "you know" and while it may be awkward at first, you will sound polished and coherent to your listeners.

6. **Remember to Use Pauses:** There are few things with more impact on the listener in a speech than a well-placed pause.

   A pause that follows a call to action, a touching story you just shared or a key point in your overall message.

   A pause is not long, 2-3 seconds is more than enough yet it seems like an eternity of silence. Make friends with that silence and allow your listener to digest your strong messages and catch up and come along for the rest of the ride.

7. **Practice Slow and Deep Breathing:** There is nothing more natural than taking a quiet deep breath

   It relaxes you and your listeners and allows your voice to speak clearly, professionally, and with purpose.

8. **Memorize your opening.** Plato said,

"The beginning is the most important part of the work".

And so it is with public speaking. The first words you express will make a lasting impression and set the tone for the rest of your speech.

9. **Don't Apologize for Anything:** If you forget something, or if you repeat something, or simply feel unprepared, do your best but do not apologize as it brings attention to something that must have gone wrong.

The audience usually never notices until your apology which then brings it to surface!

10. **Feign Confidence Until It Comes:** In an advanced public speaking course in California years ago, the instructor surprised us with this advice.

"Fake your confidence until it becomes real!" If you are nervous, hide it with deep breathing, a smile and all previous 9 tips.

11. **Get a good introduction:** Write your own bio and introduction. Build credibility with some of your previous achievements, but keep it brief. Add a little humour if you can.

    Get someone else to read it out and introduce you – it just adds that little bit of anticipation with your audience – you want them to want to hear what you have to say.

12. **Work on the close.** A strong message to wrap up your presentation, preferably with a call to action, will make a lasting impression.

    It will also increase the number of people that you end up doing business with.

    Don't go out on a whimper – stir your audience up and make them a great offer to close the session.

So, armed with this knowledge you should practice, practice, practice!

Seriously, the more you do it the better you

will become at speaking in public.

If you know your content well, and can deliver it in an interesting, entertaining manner, you will start to love speaking in public. And guess what? People will seek you out as your reputation grows as a lively and entertaining speaker.

If it can happen to me, it can happen to you too.

Chapter Nine – Leveraging Your Talk.

'Most people would rather be in the box, than giving the Eulogy'

Jerry Seinfeld is credited with the above quote, but now, dear reader, you are not afraid of speaking in public, right? Right!

So now you can give a one or two hour presentation without any fear, and you've got a few well-rehearsed ad-libs and jokes or true stories that are funny to weave into your presentation, then you're ready to leverage your new found skills by video recording some of your speeches.

The first thing to keep in mind is that this does not have to be a 'Hollywood' or 'Broadcast' quality production.

People do not expect that. It does have to be an acceptable quality, but these days it is almost impossible to produce anything less, due to the leaps and bounds made in recent years in video camera technology.

When I started getting involved in video production, in the early 1990's, we were using tape and once you went past the second generation (copies of the original footage) the quality of the finished product started to quickly reduce to the point where it was not of acceptable quality.

Today, with digital recording, there is no such degradation of quality of the footage.

You can now buy a really good digital camcorder for under $500, editing software for under $100 and a wireless microphone for under $200, so for considerably less than $1,000 you can be a film producer, just like me! (Although I did spend a lot more on a camera and a professional grade wireless microphone, lighting and other 'toys' but you don't need to for these purposes.)

Here's the method:

- Set up the equipment at the back of the venue facing you
- Get a buddy to come along to operate the camera and keep it focused on you.
- Speak to the audience/camera during

your presentation

- Get your camera operator to keep the recording going (to get continuous audio) but shoot some footage of the audience at times to use later.

- Edit the results into a series of clips of less than 15 minutes (2 to 5 minutes is fine to start with).

- Create a free YouTube account.

- Upload your clip(s) to this account

- When your clip has been processed by YouTube, go to your account and right click on the video to grab the embed code.

- Go to the 'back office' of your website and paste the embed code to post your video clip on your own website.

Now you are at a junction in the road where you can leave it at that and simply use the footage on your site to promote future presentations, or you can go to the next step, and turn your video footage into a DVD that you can either sell and make money from your seminars, or even give away as souvenirs to those who attended. (Yes, they are that cheap to produce that you can afford to give them away!)

Now you can promote your videos to your clients, prospects, contacts etc... through:

1. Your Newsletter
2. Your Website
3. Your Facebook page
4. Your Twitter Account
5. Your Linked-In page

Got an iPod/iPhone?

Why not record some business advice onto tape and upload it to iTunes as a podcast?

If you've done the above, you already have the raw materials. If you have video-taped a seminar you can extract the soundtrack and produce a CD which can also be created as an MP3 file and downloaded from iTunes as a podcast. It's free to upload an MP3 file to iTunes and you can make the speech available to the next generation of entrepreneurs via the internet.

I started to produce a passive income from my consulting work by renting a recording studio, writing a script and reading it into the microphone, where a sound engineer was monitoring the recording and produced a master audio CD for me.

I then made copies myself, in the days before I used a mass-production company to produce all my DVDs and Audio CDs.

Today I use a high end automated production facility in the USA where I can get short run productions done for between $1 and $2 per copy (plus shipping) depending on the quantity.

I get a full colour cover, with bar code so it is 'retail ready' (in case Walmart ever want to carry them!) and the disc itself is printed in full colour.

I even have a full colour insert for my DVDs so I can promote my other DVDs, CDS or services inside the products, and it all comes shrink wrapped.

How good is that?

Another way to leverage your talk is to design presentations for specific niche markets that you might want to grow your practice in.

Connect with their trade association and see if they might allow you to make some presentations to their members.

Get it video recorded and off you go!

For more information on developing a niche market, I invite you to look out for my next book **'Niche or be Niched – how to grow your professional services firm through Niche Marketing'** – available in 2015.

I sincerely hope that you found this little book useful, and that you are now armed with some of the insights to help you talk your way to the top.

About the Author

Steve McIntyre-Smith lives in Toronto, Canada.

For over 35 years he has been involved in the public accounting field.

From office junior to Partner, from buyer to seller, and, since 1992, as a consultant to the public accounting profession, Steve has a depth and breadth of experience in helping practitioners reach their goals.

He is the author of the CICA's 'Succession Planning Toolkit' for practitioners, a former resident columnist for the Bottom Line (for over 11 years) and an award-winning contributor to CA magazine (Let's Make a Deal, and other articles).

A popular PD course and Partner retreat leader and key-note speaker, Steve speaks from his own experiences – often with a touch of self-deprecating humour – to help you avoid all the mistakes he made!

He is recognized as one of North America's

leading consultants to the accounting profession, having spoken recently in Latvia, Barbados, Las Vegas, Aspen, Charleston, Whistler, Bangladesh, Australia, the UK, and literally from coast to coast in Canada.

Online, Steve is very active, publishing a number of best selling e-books, an audio CD and a free monthly newsletter, LEDGER, covering marketing, practice management and career advice for practitioners and their staff.

In recent years he's become a movie star! - Steve has produced a range of training DVDs exclusively for the public accounting profession, covering Marketing, Buying a Practice, Best Practices and more.

His annual 'Ontario Public Accounting Salary Survey' is published every May and is used by hundreds of accounting firms across the Province to set salary levels for their staff - available free of charge, from his web site.

His first novel 'A Killing on the Exchange' made the Kindle best-sellers list (at #1 no less!).

Steve firmly believes that public accounting can be a rewarding, exciting and even sexy career.

Steve can be reached at:

Telephone: 416-627-2283

Web: www.stevemcintyresmith.com

Email: steve@mcintyre-smith.com

Useful Resources:

<u>Speaking</u>

Toastmasters…. www.toastmasters.org
Zig Ziglar……….. www.ziglar.com
Dale Carnegie… www.dalecarnegie.ca

<u>Personal Achievement</u>

Tony Robbins…. <u>www.tonyrobbins.com</u>
Brian Tracy…….. <u>www.briantracy.com</u>

<u>Video Production</u>

Bill Myers – a source for everything you need to get started in video production.

<u>www.bmyers.com</u>

Kunaki – my automated DVD producer

<u>www.kunaki.com</u>

<u>Newsletter & Email Marketing</u>

Constant Contact:

<u>www.contnntcontact.com</u>

Free Newsletter for Public Accounting Professionals

LEDGER

Sign up at www.stevemcintyresmith.com

www.ingramcontent.com/pod-product-compliance
Lightning Source LLC
Chambersburg PA
CBHW051818170526
45167CB00005B/2067